POSITIVE
MINDSET JOURNAL

for TEACHERS

A YEAR OF *HAPPY THOUGHTS, INSPIRATIONAL QUOTES,*
AND REFLECTIONS
FOR A POSITIVE TEACHING EXPERIENCE

Grace Stevens

Paperback Edition ISBN: **978 0998701936**

Manufactured in the United States of America All Rights Reserved
Red Lotus Books, Mountain House CA

Red Lotus Books

This journal belongs to :

....

School Year :

....

School :

....

" Learning is the only thing the mind never exhausts, never fears and never regrets. It is the only thing that will never fail us."

Leonardo da Vinci

How to Use This Journal

The goal of this journal is to help you connect to the parts of your teaching week that bring you joy. While there is plenty of research to support the idea that a positive classroom environment will increase student engagement and achievement, this journal isn't for your students' benefits; it's for yours. **You deserve to enjoy your teaching day!**

Teaching is a "noble profession." We choose it because we know it is important, not necessarily because we believe it will be easy. But teaching can and should be fun and rewarding.

Many years of experience in the classroom have taught me that everyone's day goes smoother when the teacher is happy. I have also learned that there are specific things that I can do to train my mind to focus on the "good stuff", seek out opportunities to make a student's, a parent's or a co-worker's day and remind myself of how awesome a privilege it really is to spend my day with children.

This journal is designed to help you take a few moments to reflect on your intentions before the work week gets rolling and it's momentum gets you into "survival mode." How will you take care of **your** needs? Who can you celebrate? Who can you thank? Taking a few minutes to write down the best parts of your day before you go home will put you in a better mental space and train your mind to be a "joy detective," focusing on the good stuff.

Training your brain to seek out things you are grateful for and inspired by is simply a habit. If you work on flexing your "happy muscle" daily, you will find it easier to connect to joy in your day and share that joy with others. This humble journal can help you do that.

Leave this journal on your desk and commit to writing in it every day for three weeks. Three weeks is all it takes to form a new habit. You will find that taking a few moments to smile and reflect every day will help turn you into a "joy detective," eager to find things in your teaching day that bring you gratitude, appreciation and smiley faces.

If you keep up this happy journaling habit, at the end of the school year, you will have a treasured keepsake of a window in time that you shared with a unique group of students. No two classes are the same, and each teaching year is different.

My hope is that this journal can help you connect in the moment, and in years to come, to the best of times, the best of your students and the best of yourself. Failing that, at least you might have a few cool doodles.

Wishing you a wonderful year, and many joy-filled moments!

Grace

P.S. This journal is a companion piece to a book I wrote called Positive Mindset Habits for Teachers - 10 Steps to Reduce Stress, Increase Student Engagement and Reignite Your Passion for Teaching. You can use this journal as a stand alone piece, but if you are serious about transforming your teaching, I think you will really enjoy the book too. You can find it on Amazon and at happy-classrooms.com

Beginning of Year Intentions

What are some ways I can ensure my students and I have the most positive classroom experience this year?

_____

_____

_____

_____

_____

Some things I already do that I love and should KEEP doing

_____

_____

_____

Some things that would be helpful to CHANGE

_____

_____

_____

_____

Some things that would be helpful to START doing

_____

_____

_____

_____

_____

_____

What are some things I love doing outside of school that I can commit to engaging in to ensure I stay energized, excited about teaching, and happy in general?

_____

_____

_____

_____

_____

_____

_____

_____

Who is going to be my "life line" in my professional life this year? Who is the person I can rely on for input, advice, a shoulder to lean on, my "safe place," or just someone to laugh and celebrate with?

_____

_____

_____

Who will be the "life lines" in my personal life?

_____

_____

_____

_____

Which colleague or colleagues can I develop a closer relationship with this year? (Can I be someone's life line?)

_____

_____

_____

_____

_____

Notes from Professional Development

What "take aways" do I have from the beginning of the year Professional Development? Which ideas can I immediately implement before they get forgotten? Which ones in particular might contribute to a more joyful classroom experience?

_____

_____

_____

_____

_____

_____

_____

_____

_____

_____

_____

_____

Notes from Professional Development

_____

_____

_____

_____

_____

_____

_____

_____

_____

_____

_____

_____

_____

_____

_____

_____

_____

Notes from Professional Development

_____

_____

_____

_____

_____

_____

_____

_____

_____

_____

_____

_____

We got this!
Let's rock this year!

> *Like the sun, a teacher enlightens a mind with their love, warmth, and light.*
>
> DEBASISH MRIDHA

Date _____

My Intention for This Week:

_____

_____

_____

Who I Can Champion This Week:

_____

3 Ways I Can Take Care of Myself This Week:

1. _____

2. _____

3. _____

The Best Three Parts of My Day:

MONDAY

_____

_____

_____

_____

TUESDAY

_____

_____

_____

_____

WEDNESDAY

_____

_____

_____

_____

The Best Three Parts of My Day:

THURSDAY

_____

_____

_____

_____

FRIDAY

_____

_____

_____

_____

Something I Am Especially Grateful For This Week:

_____

_____

_____

_____

_____

Quote of the Week

Something funny a student said, a compliment you were given, or something inspirational you read

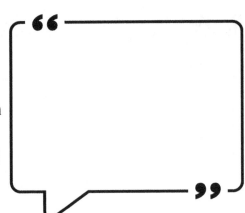

Share the Positivity

Three people I can thank or celebrate this week - in person, in writing, or by making a "day maker" phone call, text or e-mail.

1. _____ ☐

2. _____ ☐

3. _____ ☐

Check as you complete

Doodle of the Week

Get Creative! What are you thinking or feeling this week? What are you dreaming about? What or who inspired you this week? Or just draw something silly to make you smile :)

> *Teaching is not about how we see things, it is about how children see things.*
>
> KAVITA BHUPTA GHOSH

Date _____

My Intention for This Week:

_____

_____

_____

Who I Can Champion This Week:

_____

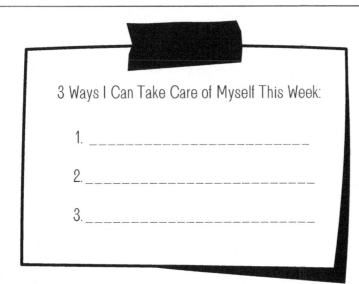

3 Ways I Can Take Care of Myself This Week:

1. _____

2. _____

3. _____

The Best Three Parts of My Day:

MONDAY

_____

_____

_____

_____

TUESDAY

_____

_____

_____

_____

WEDNESDAY

_____

_____

_____

_____

The Best Three Parts of My Day:

THURSDAY

_____

_____

_____

_____

FRIDAY

_____

_____

_____

_____

Something I Am Especially Grateful For This Week:

_____

_____

_____

_____

Quote of the Week

Something funny a student said, a compliment you were given, or something inspirational you read

Share the Positivity

Three people I can thank or celebrate this week - in person, in writing, or by making a "day maker" phone call, text or e-mail.

1. _____ ☐

2. _____ ☐

3. _____ ☐

Check as you complete

Doodle of the Week

Get Creative! What are you thinking or feeling this week? What are you dreaming about? What or who inspired you this week? Or just draw something silly to make you smile :)

> *Positive expectations are the mark*
> *of the superior personality*
>
> BRIAN TRACY

Date _____

My Intention for This Week:

_____

_____

_____

Who I Can Champion This Week:

_____

3 Ways I Can Take Care of Myself This Week:

1. _____

2. _____

3. _____

The Best Three Parts of My Day:

MONDAY

_____

_____

_____

_____

TUESDAY

_____

_____

_____

_____

WEDNESDAY

_____

_____

_____

_____

The Best Three Parts of My Day:

THURSDAY

_____

_____

_____

_____

FRIDAY

_____

_____

_____

_____

Something I Am Especially Grateful For This Week:

_____

_____

_____

_____

_____

Quote of the Week

Something funny a student said, a compliment you were given, or something inspirational you read

Share the Positivity

Three people I can thank or celebrate this week - in person, in writing, or by making a "day maker" phone call, text or e-mail.

1. _____ ☐

2. _____ ☐

3. _____ ☐

Check as you complete

Doodle of the Week

Get Creative! What are you thinking or feeling this week? What are you dreaming about? What or who inspired you this week? Or just draw something silly to make you smile :)

66 *Thousands of candles can be lighted from a single candle, and the life of the candle will not be shortened. Happiness never decreases by being shared.*

BUDDHA **99**

Date _____

My Intention for This Week:

_____

_____

_____

Who I Can Champion This Week:

_____

3 Ways I Can Take Care of Myself This Week:

1. _____

2. _____

3. _____

The Best Three Parts of My Day:

MONDAY

_____

_____

_____

_____

TUESDAY

_____

_____

_____

_____

WEDNESDAY

_____

_____

_____

_____

The Best Three Parts of My Day:

THURSDAY

_____

_____

_____

_____

FRIDAY

_____

_____

_____

_____

Something I Am Especially Grateful For This Week:

_____

_____

_____

_____

_____

Quote of the Week

Something funny a student said, a compliment you were given, or something inspirational you read

Share the Positivity

Three people I can thank or celebrate this week - in person, in writing, or by making a "day maker" phone call, text or e-mail.

1. _____ ☐

2. _____ ☐

3. _____ ☐

Check as you complete

Doodle of the Week

Get Creative! What are you thinking or feeling this week? What are you dreaming about? What or who inspired you this week? Or just draw something silly to make you smile :)

> *It is easier to build strong children*
> *than to repair broken men.*
>
> FREDERICK DOUGLAS

Date _____

My Intention for This Week:

_____

_____

_____

Who I Can Champion This Week:

_____

3 Ways I Can Take Care of Myself This Week:

1. _____

2. _____

3. _____

The Best Three Parts of My Day:

MONDAY

_____

_____

_____

_____

TUESDAY

_____

_____

_____

_____

WEDNESDAY

_____

_____

_____

_____

The Best Three Parts of My Day:

THURSDAY

_____

_____

_____

_____

FRIDAY

_____

_____

_____

_____

Something I Am Especially Grateful For This Week:

_____

_____

_____

_____

Quote of the Week

Something funny a student said, a compliment you were given, or something inspirational you read

Share the Positivity

Three people I can thank or celebrate this week - in person, in writing, or by making a "day maker" phone call, text or e-mail.

1. _____ ☐

2. _____ ☐

3. _____ ☐

Check as you complete

Doodle of the Week

Get Creative! What are you thinking or feeling this week? What are you dreaming about? What or who inspired you this week? Or just draw something silly to make you smile :)

Date _____

My Intention for This Week:

_____

_____

_____

Who I Can Champion This Week:

_____

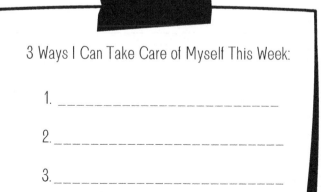

3 Ways I Can Take Care of Myself This Week:

1. _____

2. _____

3. _____

The Best Three Parts of My Day:

MONDAY

_____

_____

_____

_____

TUESDAY

_____

_____

_____

_____

WEDNESDAY

_____

_____

_____

_____

The Best Three Parts of My Day:

THURSDAY

_____

_____

_____

_____

FRIDAY

_____

_____

_____

_____

Something I Am Especially Grateful For This Week:

_____

_____

_____

_____

_____

Quote of the Week

Something funny a student said, a compliment you were given, or something inspirational you read

Share the Positivity

Three people I can thank or celebrate this week - in person, in writing, or by making a "day maker" phone call, text or e-mail.

1. _____ ☐

2. _____ ☐

3. _____ ☐

Check as you complete

Doodle of the Week

Get Creative! What are you thinking or feeling this week? What are you dreaming about? What or who inspired you this week? Or just draw something silly to make you smile :)

> *Change your thoughts and you change your world.*
>
> NORMAN VINCENT PEALE

Date _____

My Intention for This Week:

_____

_____

_____

Who I Can Champion This Week:

_____

3 Ways I Can Take Care of Myself This Week:

1. _____

2. _____

3. _____

The Best Three Parts of My Day:

MONDAY

_____

_____

_____

_____

TUESDAY

_____

_____

_____

_____

WEDNESDAY

_____

_____

_____

_____

The Best Three Parts of My Day:

THURSDAY

_____

_____

_____

_____

FRIDAY

_____

_____

_____

_____

Something I Am Especially Grateful For This Week:

_____

_____

_____

_____

_____

Quote of the Week

Something funny a student said, a compliment you were given, or something inspirational you read

Share the Positivity

Three people I can thank or celebrate this week - in person, in writing, or by making a "day maker" phone call, text or e-mail.

1. _____ ☐

2. _____ ☐

3. _____ ☐

Check as you complete

Doodle of the Week

Get Creative! What are you thinking or feeling this week? What are you dreaming about? What or who inspired you this week? Or just draw something silly to make you smile :)

> *Let us remember: One book, one pen, one child, and one teacher can change the world.*
>
> MALALA YOUSAFZAI

Date _____

My Intention for This Week:

_____

_____

_____

Who I Can Champion This Week:

_____

3 Ways I Can Take Care of Myself This Week:

1. _____

2. _____

3. _____

The Best Three Parts of My Day:

MONDAY

_____

_____

_____

_____

TUESDAY

_____

_____

_____

_____

WEDNESDAY

_____

_____

_____

_____

The Best Three Parts of My Day:

THURSDAY

_____

_____

_____

_____

FRIDAY

_____

_____

_____

_____

Something I Am Especially Grateful For This Week:

_____

_____

_____

_____

_____

Quote of the Week

Something funny a student said, a compliment you were given, or something inspirational you read

Share the Positivity

Three people I can thank or celebrate this week - in person, in writing, or by making a "day maker" phone call, text or e-mail.

1. _____ ☐

2. _____ ☐

3. _____ ☐

Check as you complete

Doodle of the Week

Get Creative! What are you thinking or feeling this week? What are you dreaming about? What or who inspired you this week? Or just draw something silly to make you smile :)

" *Happiness is not something you postpone for the future; it is something you design for the present.*

JIM ROHN

"

Date _____

My Intention for This Week:

_____

_____

_____

Who I Can Champion This Week:

_____

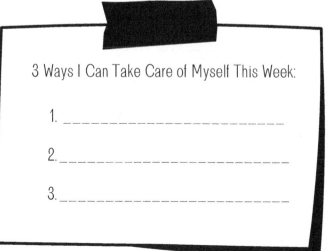

3 Ways I Can Take Care of Myself This Week:

1. _____

2. _____

3. _____

The Best Three Parts of My Day:

MONDAY

_____

_____

_____

_____

TUESDAY

_____

_____

_____

_____

WEDNESDAY

_____

_____

_____

_____

The Best Three Parts of My Day:

THURSDAY

_____

_____

_____

_____

FRIDAY

_____

_____

_____

_____

Something I Am Especially Grateful For This Week:

_____

_____

_____

_____

_____

Quote of the Week

Something funny a student said, a compliment you were given, or something inspirational you read

Share the Positivity

Three people I can thank or celebrate this week - in person, in writing, or by making a "day maker" phone call, text or e-mail.

1. _____ ☐

2. _____ ☐

3. _____ ☐

Check as you complete

Doodle of the Week

Get Creative! What are you thinking or feeling this week? What are you dreaming about? What or who inspired you this week? Or just draw something silly to make you smile :)

> *Children will not remember you for the material things you provided but for the feeling that you cherished them.*
>
> RICHARD L. EVANS

Date _____

My Intention for This Week:

_____

_____

_____

Who I Can Champion This Week:

_____

3 Ways I Can Take Care of Myself This Week:

1. _____

2. _____

3. _____

The Best Three Parts of My Day:

MONDAY

_____

_____

_____

_____

TUESDAY

_____

_____

_____

_____

WEDNESDAY

_____

_____

_____

_____

The Best Three Parts of My Day:

THURSDAY

_____

_____

_____

_____

FRIDAY

_____

_____

_____

_____

Something I Am Especially Grateful For This Week:

_____

_____

_____

_____

_____

Quote of the Week

Something funny a student said, a compliment you were given, or something inspirational you read

Share the Positivity

Three people I can thank or celebrate this week - in person, in writing, or by making a "day maker" phone call, text or e-mail.

1. _____ ☐

2. _____ ☐

3. _____ ☐

Check as you complete

Doodle of the Week

Get Creative! What are you thinking or feeling this week? What are you dreaming about? What or who inspired you this week? Or just draw something silly to make you smile :)

> *The best and most beautiful things in the world cannot be seen or even touched - they must be felt with the heart.*
>
> HELEN KELLER

Date _____

My Intention for This Week:

_____

_____

_____

Who I Can Champion This Week:

_____

3 Ways I Can Take Care of Myself This Week:

1. _____

2. _____

3. _____

The Best Three Parts of My Day:

MONDAY

_____

_____

_____

_____

TUESDAY

_____

_____

_____

WEDNESDAY

_____

_____

_____

_____

The Best Three Parts of My Day:

THURSDAY

_____

_____

_____

FRIDAY

_____

_____

_____

Something I Am Especially Grateful For This Week:

_____

_____

_____

_____

Quote of the Week

Something funny a student said, a compliment you were given, or something inspirational you read

Share the Positivity

Three people I can thank or celebrate this week - in person, in writing, or by making a "day maker" phone call, text or e-mail.

1. _____ ☐

2. _____ ☐

3. _____ ☐

Check as you complete

Doodle of the Week

Get Creative! What are you thinking or feeling this week? What are you dreaming about? What or who inspired you this week? Or just draw something silly to make you smile :)

> *When the sun is shining I can do anything; no mountain is too high, no trouble too difficult to overcome.*
>
> WILMA RUDOLPH

Date _____

My Intention for This Week:

_____

_____

_____

Who I Can Champion This Week:

_____

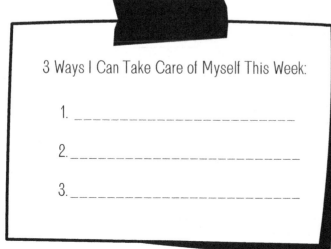

3 Ways I Can Take Care of Myself This Week:

1. _____

2. _____

3. _____

The Best Three Parts of My Day:

MONDAY

_____

_____

_____

_____

TUESDAY

_____

_____

_____

_____

WEDNESDAY

_____

_____

_____

_____

The Best Three Parts of My Day:

THURSDAY

_____

_____

_____

_____

FRIDAY

_____

_____

_____

_____

Something I Am Especially Grateful For This Week:

_____

_____

_____

_____

_____

Quote of the Week

Something funny a student said, a compliment you were given, or something inspirational you read

Share the Positivity

Three people I can thank or celebrate this week - in person, in writing, or by making a "day maker" phone call, text or e-mail.

1. _____ ☐

2. _____ ☐

3. _____ ☐

Check as you complete

Doodle of the Week

Get Creative! What are you thinking or feeling this week? What are you dreaming about? What or who inspired you this week? Or just draw something silly to make you smile :)

> *Correction does much, but*
> *encouragement does more.*
>
> Johann Wolfgang von Goethe

Date _____

My Intention for This Week:

_____

_____

_____

Who I Can Champion This Week:

_____

3 Ways I Can Take Care of Myself This Week:

1. _____

2. _____

3. _____

The Best Three Parts of My Day:

MONDAY

_____

_____

_____

_____

TUESDAY

_____

_____

_____

_____

WEDNESDAY

_____

_____

_____

_____

The Best Three Parts of My Day:

THURSDAY

_____

_____

_____

_____

FRIDAY

_____

_____

_____

_____

Something I Am Especially Grateful For This Week:

_____

_____

_____

_____

_____

Quote of the Week

Something funny a student said, a compliment you were given, or something inspirational you read

Share the Positivity

Three people I can thank or celebrate this week - in person, in writing, or by making a "day maker" phone call, text or e-mail.

1. _____ ☐

2. _____ ☐

3. _____ ☐

Check as you complete

Doodle of the Week

Get Creative! What are you thinking or feeling this week? What are you dreaming about? What or who inspired you this week? Or just draw something silly to make you smile :)

The mediocre teacher tells. The good teacher explains. The superior teacher demonstrates. The great teacher inspires.

WILLIAM ARTHUR WARDE

Date _____

My Intention for This Week:

_____

_____

_____

Who I Can Champion This Week:

_____

3 Ways I Can Take Care of Myself This Week:

1. _____

2. _____

3. _____

The Best Three Parts of My Day:

MONDAY

_____

_____

_____

_____

TUESDAY

_____

_____

_____

_____

WEDNESDAY

_____

_____

_____

_____

The Best Three Parts of My Day:

THURSDAY

_____

_____

_____

_____

FRIDAY

_____

_____

_____

_____

Something I Am Especially Grateful For This Week:

_____

_____

_____

_____

Quote of the Week

Something funny a student said, a compliment you were given, or something inspirational you read

Share the Positivity

Three people I can thank or celebrate this week - in person, in writing, or by making a "day maker" phone call, text or e-mail.

1. _____ ☐

2. _____ ☐

3. _____ ☐

Check as you complete

Doodle of the Week

Get Creative! What are you thinking or feeling this week? What are you dreaming about? What or who inspired you this week? Or just draw something silly to make you smile :)

> *Our greatest natural resource is the minds of our children.*
>
> WALT DISNEY

Date _____

My Intention for This Week:

_____

_____

_____

Who I Can Champion This Week:

_____

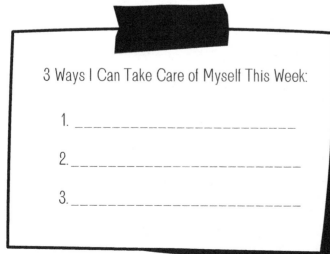

3 Ways I Can Take Care of Myself This Week:

1. _____

2. _____

3. _____

The Best Three Parts of My Day:

MONDAY

_____

_____

_____

_____

TUESDAY

_____

_____

_____

_____

WEDNESDAY

_____

_____

_____

_____

The Best Three Parts of My Day:

THURSDAY

_____

_____

_____

_____

FRIDAY

_____

_____

_____

_____

Something I Am Especially Grateful For This Week:

_____

_____

_____

_____

_____

Quote of the Week

Something funny a student said, a compliment you were given, or something inspirational you read

Share the Positivity

Three people I can thank or celebrate this week - in person, in writing, or by making a "day maker" phone call, text or e-mail.

1. _____ ☐

2. _____ ☐

3. _____ ☐

Check as you complete

Doodle of the Week

Get Creative! What are you thinking or feeling this week? What are you dreaming about? What or who inspired you this week? Or just draw something silly to make you smile :)

> *Try to be a rainbow in someone's cloud.*
>
> MAYA ANGELOU

Date _____

My Intention for This Week:

_____

_____

_____

Who I Can Champion This Week:

_____

3 Ways I Can Take Care of Myself This Week:

1. _____

2. _____

3. _____

The Best Three Parts of My Day:

MONDAY

TUESDAY

WEDNESDAY

The Best Three Parts of My Day:

THURSDAY

_____

_____

_____

_____

FRIDAY

_____

_____

_____

_____

Something I Am Especially Grateful For This Week:

_____

_____

_____

_____

_____

Quote of the Week

Something funny a student said, a compliment you were given, or something inspirational you read

Share the Positivity

Three people I can thank or celebrate this week - in person, in writing, or by making a "day maker" phone call, text or e-mail.

1. _____ ☐

2. _____ ☐

3. _____ ☐

Check as you complete

Doodle of the Week

Get Creative! What are you thinking or feeling this week? What are you dreaming about? What or who inspired you this week? Or just draw something silly to make you smile :)

"

Don't struggle to be a better teacher than everyone else. Simply be a better teacher than you ever thought you could be.

ROBERT JOHN
MEEHAN **"**

Date _____

My Intention for This Week:

_____

_____

_____

Who I Can Champion This Week:

_____

3 Ways I Can Take Care of Myself This Week:

1. _____

2. _____

3. _____

The Best Three Parts of My Day:

MONDAY

_____

_____

_____

_____

TUESDAY

_____

_____

_____

_____

WEDNESDAY

_____

_____

_____

_____

The Best Three Parts of My Day:

THURSDAY

_____

_____

_____

_____

FRIDAY

_____

_____

_____

_____

Something I Am Especially Grateful For This Week:

_____

_____

_____

_____

_____

Quote of the Week

Something funny a student said, a compliment you were given, or something inspirational you read

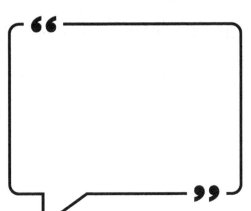

Share the Positivity

Three people I can thank or celebrate this week - in person, in writing, or by making a "day maker" phone call, text or e-mail.

1. _____ ☐

2. _____ ☐

3. _____ ☐

Check as you complete

Doodle of the Week

Get Creative! What are you thinking or feeling this week? What are you dreaming about? What or who inspired you this week? Or just draw something silly to make you smile :)

> *The fruits of your labors may be reaped two generations from now. Trust, even when you don't see the results.*
>
> HENRI NOUWEN

Date _____

My Intention for This Week:

_____

_____

_____

Who I Can Champion This Week:

_____

3 Ways I Can Take Care of Myself This Week:

1. _____

2. _____

3. _____

The Best Three Parts of My Day:

MONDAY

_____

_____

_____

_____

TUESDAY

_____

_____

_____

_____

WEDNESDAY

_____

_____

_____

_____

The Best Three Parts of My Day:

THURSDAY

_____

_____

_____

_____

FRIDAY

_____

_____

_____

_____

Something I Am Especially Grateful For This Week:

_____

_____

_____

_____

_____

Quote of the Week

Something funny a student said, a compliment you were given, or something inspirational you read

Share the Positivity

Three people I can thank or celebrate this week - in person, in writing, or by making a "day maker" phone call, text or e-mail.

1. _____ ☐

2. _____ ☐

3. _____ ☐

Check as you complete

Doodle of the Week

Get Creative! What are you thinking or feeling this week? What are you dreaming about? What or who inspired you this week? Or just draw something silly to make you smile :)

Date _____

My Intention for This Week:

_____

_____

_____

Who I Can Champion This Week:

_____

3 Ways I Can Take Care of Myself This Week:

1. _____

2. _____

3. _____

The Best Three Parts of My Day:

MONDAY

_____

_____

_____

_____

TUESDAY

_____

_____

_____

_____

WEDNESDAY

_____

_____

_____

_____

The Best Three Parts of My Day:

THURSDAY

_____

_____

_____

_____

FRIDAY

_____

_____

_____

_____

Something I Am Especially Grateful For This Week:

_____

_____

_____

_____

_____

Quote of the Week

Something funny a student said, a compliment you were given, or something inspirational you read

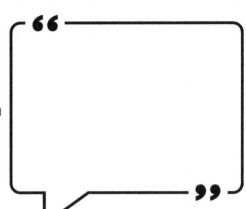

Share the Positivity

Three people I can thank or celebrate this week - in person, in writing, or by making a "day maker" phone call, text or e-mail.

1. _____ ☐

2. _____ ☐

3. _____ ☐

Check as you complete

Doodle of the Week

Get Creative! What are you thinking or feeling this week? What are you dreaming about? What or who inspired you this week? Or just draw something silly to make you smile :)

> *There are only two ways to live: you can live as if nothing is a miracle, or you can live as if everything is a miracle.*
>
> ALBERT EINSTEIN

Date _____

My Intention for This Week:

_____

_____

_____

Who I Can Champion This Week:

_____

3 Ways I Can Take Care of Myself This Week:

1. _____

2. _____

3. _____

The Best Three Parts of My Day:

MONDAY

_____

_____

_____

_____

TUESDAY

_____

_____

_____

_____

WEDNESDAY

_____

_____

_____

_____

The Best Three Parts of My Day:

THURSDAY

_____

_____

_____

_____

FRIDAY

_____

_____

_____

_____

Something I Am Especially Grateful For This Week:

_____

_____

_____

_____

_____

Quote of the Week

Something funny a student said, a compliment you were given, or something inspirational you read

Share the Positivity

Three people I can thank or celebrate this week - in person, in writing, or by making a "day maker" phone call, text or e-mail.

1. _____ ☐

2. _____ ☐

3. _____ ☐

Check as you complete

Doodle of the Week

Get Creative! What are you thinking or feeling this week? What are you dreaming about? What or who inspired you this week? Or just draw something silly to make you smile :)

> *Feeling gratitude and not expressing it is like wrapping a present and not giving it.*
>
> WILLIAM ARTHUR WARD

Date _____

My Intention for This Week:

_____

_____

_____

Who I Can Champion This Week:

_____

3 Ways I Can Take Care of Myself This Week:

1. _____

2. _____

3. _____

The Best Three Parts of My Day:

MONDAY

_____

_____

_____

_____

TUESDAY

_____

_____

_____

WEDNESDAY

_____

_____

_____

_____

The Best Three Parts of My Day:

THURSDAY

_____

_____

_____

_____

FRIDAY

_____

_____

_____

Something I Am Especially Grateful For This Week:

_____

_____

_____

_____

_____

Quote of the Week

Something funny a student said, a compliment you were given, or something inspirational you read

Share the Positivity

Three people I can thank or celebrate this week - in person, in writing, or by making a "day maker" phone call, text or e-mail.

1. _____ ☐

2. _____ ☐

3. _____ ☐

Check as you complete

Doodle of the Week

Get Creative! What are you thinking or feeling this week? What are you dreaming about? What or who inspired you this week? Or just draw something silly to make you smile :)

> *What salt is to food,*
> *passion is to teaching.*
>
> KAVITA BHUPTA GHOSH

Date _____

My Intention for This Week:

_____

_____

_____

Who I Can Champion This Week:

_____

3 Ways I Can Take Care of Myself This Week:

1. _____

2. _____

3. _____

The Best Three Parts of My Day:

MONDAY

_____

_____

_____

_____

TUESDAY

_____

_____

_____

_____

WEDNESDAY

_____

_____

_____

_____

The Best Three Parts of My Day:

THURSDAY

_____

_____

_____

_____

FRIDAY

_____

_____

_____

_____

Something I Am Especially Grateful For This Week:

_____

_____

_____

_____

_____

Quote of the Week

Something funny a student said, a compliment you were given, or something inspirational you read

Share the Positivity

Three people I can thank or celebrate this week - in person, in writing, or by making a "day maker" phone call, text or e-mail.

1. _____ ☐

2. _____ ☐

3. _____ ☐

Check as you complete

Doodle of the Week

Get Creative! What are you thinking or feeling this week? What are you dreaming about? What or who inspired you this week? Or just draw something silly to make you smile :)

> *The most valuable resource teachers have is*
> *each other. Without collaboration, our*
> *growth is limited to our own perspective.*
>
> ROBERT JOHN MEEHAN

Date _____

My Intention for This Week:

_____

_____

_____

Who I Can Champion This Week:

_____

3 Ways I Can Take Care of Myself This Week:

1. _____

2. _____

3. _____

The Best Three Parts of My Day:

MONDAY

_____

_____

_____

_____

TUESDAY

_____

_____

_____

WEDNESDAY

_____

_____

_____

_____

The Best Three Parts of My Day:

THURSDAY

_____

_____

_____

_____

FRIDAY

_____

_____

_____

_____

Something I Am Especially Grateful For This Week:

_____

_____

_____

_____

_____

Quote of the Week

Something funny a student said, a compliment you were given, or something inspirational you read

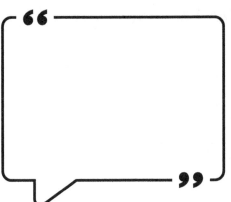

Share the Positivity

Three people I can thank or celebrate this week - in person, in writing, or by making a "day maker" phone call, text or e-mail.

1. _____ ☐

2. _____ ☐

3. _____ ☐

Check as you complete

Doodle of the Week

Get Creative! What are you thinking or feeling this week? What are you dreaming about? What or who inspired you this week? Or just draw something silly to make you smile :)

> *We cannot always do great things.*
> *But we can do small things with*
> *great love.*
> MOTHER TERESA

Date _____

My Intention for This Week:

_____

_____

_____

Who I Can Champion This Week:

_____

3 Ways I Can Take Care of Myself This Week:

1. _____

2. _____

3. _____

The Best Three Parts of My Day:

MONDAY

_____

_____

_____

TUESDAY

_____

_____

_____

WEDNESDAY

_____

_____

_____

The Best Three Parts of My Day:

THURSDAY

_____

_____

_____

_____

FRIDAY

_____

_____

_____

_____

Something I Am Especially Grateful For This Week:

_____

_____

_____

_____

Quote of the Week

Something funny a student said, a compliment you were given, or something inspirational you read

Share the Positivity

Three people I can thank or celebrate this week - in person, in writing, or by making a "day maker" phone call, text or e-mail.

1. _____ ☐

2. _____ ☐

3. _____ ☐

Check as you complete

Doodle of the Week

Get Creative! What are you thinking or feeling this week? What are you dreaming about? What or who inspired you this week? Or just draw something silly to make you smile :)

> *I've come to the frightening conclusion that I am the decisive element in the classroom. It's my personal approach that creates the climate. It's my daily mood that makes the weather.*
>
> HAIM G. GINOTT

Date _____

My Intention for This Week:

_____

_____

_____

Who I Can Champion This Week:

_____

3 Ways I Can Take Care of Myself This Week:

1. _____

2. _____

3. _____

The Best Three Parts of My Day:

MONDAY

_____

_____

_____

TUESDAY

_____

_____

_____

WEDNESDAY

_____

_____

_____

The Best Three Parts of My Day:

THURSDAY

_____

_____

_____

_____

FRIDAY

_____

_____

_____

_____

Something I Am Especially Grateful For This Week:

_____

_____

_____

_____

Quote of the Week

Something funny a student said, a
compliment you were given, or
something inspirational you read

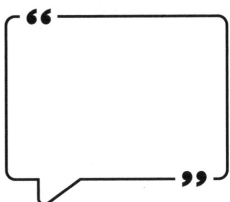

Share the Positivity

Three people I can thank or celebrate this week - in person, in writing, or
by making a "day maker" phone call, text or e-mail.

1. _____ ☐

2. _____ ☐

3. _____ ☐

Check as you complete

Doodle of the Week

Get Creative! What are you
thinking or feeling this
week? What are you
dreaming about? What or
who inspired you this
week? Or just draw
something silly to make you
smile :)

> *Technology is just a tool. In terms of getting kids working together and motivating them, the teacher is the most important.*
>
> BILL GATES

Date _____

My Intention for This Week:

_____

_____

_____

Who I Can Champion This Week:

_____

3 Ways I Can Take Care of Myself This Week:

1. _____

2. _____

3. _____

The Best Three Parts of My Day:

MONDAY

_____

_____

_____

_____

TUESDAY

_____

_____

_____

_____

WEDNESDAY

_____

_____

_____

_____

The Best Three Parts of My Day:

THURSDAY

_____

_____

_____

_____

FRIDAY

_____

_____

_____

_____

Something I Am Especially Grateful For This Week:

_____

_____

_____

_____

Quote of the Week

Something funny a student said, a compliment you were given, or something inspirational you read

Share the Positivity

Three people I can thank or celebrate this week - in person, in writing, or by making a "day maker" phone call, text or e-mail.

1. _____ ☐

2. _____ ☐

3. _____ ☐

Check as you complete

Doodle of the Week

Get Creative! What are you thinking or feeling this week? What are you dreaming about? What or who inspired you this week? Or just draw something silly to make you smile :)

> *It is the supreme art of the teacher*
> *to awaken joy in creative*
> *expression and knowledge.*
>
> ALBERT EINSTEIN

Date _____

My Intention for This Week:

_____

_____

_____

Who I Can Champion This Week:

_____

3 Ways I Can Take Care of Myself This Week:

1. _____

2. _____

3. _____

The Best Three Parts of My Day:

MONDAY

_____

_____

_____

_____

TUESDAY

_____

_____

_____

_____

WEDNESDAY

_____

_____

_____

_____

The Best Three Parts of My Day:

THURSDAY

_____

_____

_____

_____

FRIDAY

_____

_____

_____

_____

Something I Am Especially Grateful For This Week:

_____

_____

_____

_____

_____

Quote of the Week

Something funny a student said, a compliment you were given, or something inspirational you read

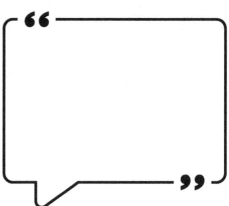

Share the Positivity

Three people I can thank or celebrate this week - in person, in writing, or by making a "day maker" phone call, text or e-mail.

1. _____ ☐

2. _____ ☐

3. _____ ☐

Check as you complete

Doodle of the Week

Get Creative! What are you thinking or feeling this week? What are you dreaming about? What or who inspired you this week? Or just draw something silly to make you smile :)

> *Teach by teaching, not by correcting.*
>
> MARIA MONTESSORI

Date _____

My Intention for This Week:

_____

_____

_____

Who I Can Champion This Week:

_____

3 Ways I Can Take Care of Myself This Week:

1. _____

2. _____

3. _____

The Best Three Parts of My Day:

MONDAY

_____

_____

_____

_____

TUESDAY

_____

_____

_____

_____

WEDNESDAY

_____

_____

_____

_____

The Best Three Parts of My Day:

THURSDAY

_____

_____

_____

_____

FRIDAY

_____

_____

_____

_____

Something I Am Especially Grateful For This Week:

_____

_____

_____

_____

Quote of the Week

Something funny a student said, a compliment you were given, or something inspirational you read

Share the Positivity

Three people I can thank or celebrate this week - in person, in writing, or by making a "day maker" phone call, text or e-mail.

1. _____ ☐

2. _____ ☐

3. _____ ☐

Check as you complete

Doodle of the Week

Get Creative! What are you thinking or feeling this week? What are you dreaming about? What or who inspired you this week? Or just draw something silly to make you smile :)

> *Each day of our lives we make deposits in the memory banks of our children.*
>
> CHARLES R. SWINDOLL

Date _____

My Intention for This Week:

_____

_____

_____

Who I Can Champion This Week:

_____

3 Ways I Can Take Care of Myself This Week:

1. _____

2. _____

3. _____

The Best Three Parts of My Day:

MONDAY

_____

_____

_____

_____

TUESDAY

_____

_____

_____

_____

WEDNESDAY

_____

_____

_____

_____

The Best Three Parts of My Day:

THURSDAY

_____

_____

_____

_____

FRIDAY

_____

_____

_____

_____

Something I Am Especially Grateful For This Week:

_____

_____

_____

_____

_____

Quote of the Week

Something funny a student said, a compliment you were given, or something inspirational you read

Share the Positivity

Three people I can thank or celebrate this week - in person, in writing, or by making a "day maker" phone call, text or e-mail.

1. _____ ☐

2. _____ ☐

3. _____ ☐

Check as you complete

Doodle of the Week

Get Creative! What are you thinking or feeling this week? What are you dreaming about? What or who inspired you this week? Or just draw something silly to make you smile :)

I like a teacher who gives you something to take home to think about besides homework.

LILY TOMLIN

Date _____

My Intention for This Week:

_____

_____

_____

Who I Can Champion This Week:

_____

3 Ways I Can Take Care of Myself This Week:

1. _____

2. _____

3. _____

The Best Three Parts of My Day:

MONDAY

_____

_____

_____

_____

TUESDAY

_____

_____

_____

_____

WEDNESDAY

_____

_____

_____

_____

The Best Three Parts of My Day:

THURSDAY

_____

_____

_____

_____

FRIDAY

_____

_____

_____

_____

Something I Am Especially Grateful For This Week:

_____

_____

_____

_____

_____

Quote of the Week

Something funny a student said, a compliment you were given, or something inspirational you read

Share the Positivity

Three people I can thank or celebrate this week - in person, in writing, or by making a "day maker" phone call, text or e-mail.

1. _____

2. _____

3. _____

Check as you complete

Doodle of the Week

Get Creative! What are you thinking or feeling this week? What are you dreaming about? What or who inspired you this week? Or just draw something silly to make you smile :)

> *Be happy for this moment. This moment is your life.*
>
> OMAR KHAYYAM

Date _____

My Intention for This Week:

_____

_____

_____

Who I Can Champion This Week:

_____

3 Ways I Can Take Care of Myself This Week:

1. _____

2. _____

3. _____

The Best Three Parts of My Day:

MONDAY

TUESDAY

WEDNESDAY

The Best Three Parts of My Day:

THURSDAY

_____

_____

_____

_____

FRIDAY

_____

_____

_____

_____

Something I Am Especially Grateful For This Week:

_____

_____

_____

_____

_____

Quote of the Week

Something funny a student said, a compliment you were given, or something inspirational you read

Share the Positivity

Three people I can thank or celebrate this week - in person, in writing, or by making a "day maker" phone call, text or e-mail.

1. _____ ☐

2. _____ ☐

3. _____ ☐

Check as you complete

Doodle of the Week

Get Creative! What are you thinking or feeling this week? What are you dreaming about? What or who inspired you this week? Or just draw something silly to make you smile :)

Teachers who are crazy enough to think they can change the world, usually do.

UNKNOWN

Date _____

My Intention for This Week:

_____

_____

_____

Who I Can Champion This Week:

_____

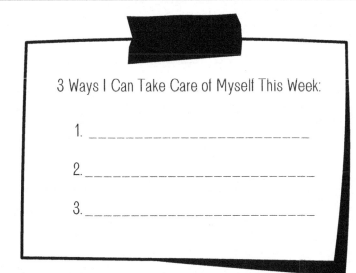

3 Ways I Can Take Care of Myself This Week:

1. _____

2. _____

3. _____

The Best Three Parts of My Day:

MONDAY

_____

_____

_____

_____

TUESDAY

_____

_____

_____

_____

WEDNESDAY

_____

_____

_____

_____

The Best Three Parts of My Day:

THURSDAY

_____

_____

_____

_____

FRIDAY

_____

_____

_____

_____

Something I Am Especially Grateful For This Week:

_____

_____

_____

_____

_____

Quote of the Week

Something funny a student said, a compliment you were given, or something inspirational you read

Share the Positivity

Three people I can thank or celebrate this week - in person, in writing, or by making a "day maker" phone call, text or e-mail.

1. _____ ☐

2. _____ ☐

3. _____ ☐

Check as you complete

Doodle of the Week

Get Creative! What are you thinking or feeling this week? What are you dreaming about? What or who inspired you this week? Or just draw something silly to make you smile :)

Education is the most powerful weapon which you can use to change the world.

NELSON MANDELA

Date _____

My Intention for This Week:

_____

_____

_____

Who I Can Champion This Week:

_____

3 Ways I Can Take Care of Myself This Week:

1. _____

2. _____

3. _____

The Best Three Parts of My Day:

MONDAY

_____

_____

_____

TUESDAY

_____

_____

_____

WEDNESDAY

_____

_____

_____

The Best Three Parts of My Day:

THURSDAY

_____

_____

_____

_____

FRIDAY

_____

_____

_____

_____

Something I Am Especially Grateful For This Week:

_____

_____

_____

_____

_____

Quote of the Week

Something funny a student said, a compliment you were given, or something inspirational you read

Share the Positivity

Three people I can thank or celebrate this week - in person, in writing, or by making a "day maker" phone call, text or e-mail.

1. _____ ☐

2. _____ ☐

3. _____ ☐

Check as you complete

Doodle of the Week

Get Creative! What are you thinking or feeling this week? What are you dreaming about? What or who inspired you this week? Or just draw something silly to make you smile :)

"

Success is not the key to happiness.
Happiness is the key to success. If you love
what you are doing, you will be successful.

ALBERT SCHWEITZER

"

Date _____

My Intention for This Week:

_____

_____

_____

Who I Can Champion This Week:

_____

3 Ways I Can Take Care of Myself This Week:

1. _____

2. _____

3. _____

The Best Three Parts of My Day:

MONDAY

_____

_____

_____

_____

TUESDAY

_____

_____

_____

_____

WEDNESDAY

_____

_____

_____

_____

The Best Three Parts of My Day:

THURSDAY

_____

_____

_____

_____

FRIDAY

_____

_____

_____

_____

Something I Am Especially Grateful For This Week:

_____

_____

_____

_____

_____

Quote of the Week

Something funny a student said, a compliment you were given, or something inspirational you read

Share the Positivity

Three people I can thank or celebrate this week - in person, in writing, or by making a "day maker" phone call, text or e-mail.

1. _____ ☐
2. _____ ☐
3. _____ ☐

Check as you complete

Doodle of the Week

Get Creative! What are you thinking or feeling this week? What are you dreaming about? What or who inspired you this week? Or just draw something silly to make you smile :)

> *Our job is not to prepare our students for something. Our job is to help our students prepare themselves for anything.*
>
> A.J. JULIANI

Date _____

My Intention for This Week:

_____

_____

_____

Who I Can Champion This Week:

_____

3 Ways I Can Take Care of Myself This Week:

1. _____

2. _____

3. _____

The Best Three Parts of My Day:

MONDAY

_____

_____

_____

_____

TUESDAY

_____

_____

_____

_____

WEDNESDAY

_____

_____

_____

_____

The Best Three Parts of My Day:

THURSDAY

_____

_____

_____

_____

FRIDAY

_____

_____

_____

_____

Something I Am Especially Grateful For This Week:

_____

_____

_____

_____

_____

Quote of the Week

Something funny a student said, a compliment you were given, or something inspirational you read

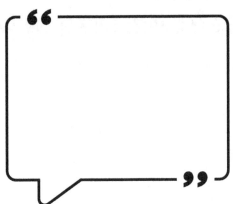

Share the Positivity

Three people I can thank or celebrate this week - in person, in writing, or by making a "day maker" phone call, text or e-mail.

1. _____ ☐

2. _____ ☐

3. _____ ☐

Check as you complete

Doodle of the Week

Get Creative! What are you thinking or feeling this week? What are you dreaming about? What or who inspired you this week? Or just draw something silly to make you smile :)

> *If kids come to us from strong, healthy, functioning families, it makes our job easier. If they don't, it makes our job more important.*
>
> BARBARA COLOROSE

Date _____

My Intention for This Week:

_____

_____

_____

Who I Can Champion This Week:

_____

3 Ways I Can Take Care of Myself This Week:

1. _____

2. _____

3. _____

The Best Three Parts of My Day:

MONDAY

_____

_____

_____

_____

TUESDAY

_____

_____

_____

_____

WEDNESDAY

_____

_____

_____

_____

The Best Three Parts of My Day:

THURSDAY

_____

_____

_____

_____

FRIDAY

_____

_____

_____

_____

Something I Am Especially Grateful For This Week:

_____

_____

_____

_____

Quote of the Week

Something funny a student said, a compliment you were given, or something inspirational you read

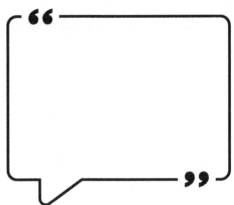

Share the Positivity

Three people I can thank or celebrate this week - in person, in writing, or by making a "day maker" phone call, text or e-mail.

1. _____ ☐

2. _____ ☐

3. _____ ☐

Check as you complete

Doodle of the Week

Get Creative! What are you thinking or feeling this week? What are you dreaming about? What or who inspired you this week? Or just draw something silly to make you smile :)

End of Year Reflections

What are some ways I grew this year?

_____

_____

_____

_____

_____

What was the most pleasant surprise of my year?

_____

_____

_____

Who did I grow closer to this year in a way I hadn't expected?

_____

_____

_____

Who is someone who made my life easier this year that I can thank?

_____

What are some ways that I can regroup and recharge this summer?

_____

_____

_____

_____

What do I need to learn more about or which resources (websites, books, podcasts) can I invest time in that will set me up for success next year?

_____

_____

_____

_____

_____

_____

_____

In ten years from now, which students will I still remember who brought me the most joy, made me laugh or caused me to stretch the most?

_____

_____

_____

_____

_____

_____

What will I remember most about this year?

_____

_____

_____

_____

_____

_____

_____

This Year's All Stars

Use this space to paste a picture of your colleagues or your class

"A hundred years from now it will not matter what my bank account was, the sort of house I lived in, or the kind of car I drove... but the world may be different because I was important in the life of a child."

Unknown

Good Karma

AI thank you from the bottom of my heart for all that you do for children and education. It is an important and noble endeavor to educate minds and build a solid, bright, hopeful foundation for our collective future. At the heart of it all, are the unsung heroes who show up in classrooms every day.
The teachers.

Please Help Spread the Love and Positivity

If you enjoyed this journal, please consider gifting a copy to a fellow teacher. Or ask your admin to buy copies for the entire staff :)

Also, if you would leave an honest review on Amazon it will help people find this book, and know if it is for them. Every single review is important to me, even if it's just two lines.

You May Also Love

This journal is a companion piece to a book called Positive Mindset Habits For Teachers - 10 Steps to Reduce Stress, Increase Student Engagement and Reignite Your Passion For Teaching. It's packed with the latest research on positive psychology, exercises, and practical advice on how to reduce teacher overwhelm and stress and put passion and joy in your classroom and your life. Find out more at happy-classrooms.com or check it out on Amazon.

Other Versions of this Journal

There are three versions of this journal available. Feedback I received is that it would be fun to have different journal covers for different school years, so I sometimes mix it up! There is also a version designed especially for Special Education teachers. All three versions of the journal are available on Amazon, and other booksellers.

Latest Book to Transform Your Teaching

About the Author

My mission is simple:

"Happier Classrooms for Students and Teachers"

Grace is a public school teacher in Northern California. A self confessed "joy junkie", she is the author of the One New Habit book series as well as Positive Mindset Habits for Teachers. Grace lived and studied in four countries before making California her home. She stepped away from a successful corporate career when she realized that hanging around young, inquiring minds was a really great way to spend her day. She holds credentials to teach two foreign languages that she has yet to use, and is also a Certified NLP (Neuro- Linguistic Programming) Practitioner. More importantly, she is a mom to two adult children, many fourth-graders, and one too many cats. They all agree she has a contagious love of learning and a very happy classroom.

Made in the USA
Monee, IL
05 August 2021

75015471R00095